LEARN ABOUT FRANCE

For Kids

This Book Belongs to:

_____

Learn About France Contents

Learn About France Contents

France is in Western Europe and is bordered by Belgium, Luxembourg, Germany, Switzerland, Italy, Spain and Andorra. That's a lot of neighbours!

Mainland France is divided into 27 regions and 101 departments. Of the 101 departments, 5 ROM ('régions d'outre mer' meaning overseas territories) belong to France.

The five overseas departments of France are:
- French Guyana in South America
- Guadeloupe, an island in the Caribbean
- Martinique, an island in the Caribbean,
- Mayotte, an island in the Indian Ocean in Africa
- La Réunion, another Indian Ocean island in Africa

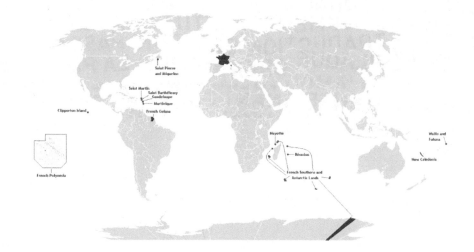

The Language

French is the only official language in France and is the first language of 88% of the population. And since France doesn't officially recognise any other language, most of those who speak minority languages also speak French.

Common Expressions

Bonjour (bon - jure)= Hello, Good morning
Au revoir (o rev-wah)= Goodbye
Oui (we)= yes
Non (no)= no
Fille (fee-ya)= Girl
Garçon (gar-son)= Boy
Je m'appelle (je-mapell)= My name is
S'il vous plaît (sil-voo-play)= Please
Merci (mare-see)= Thank you
Bonsoir (bon-swa)= Good evening
Bonne Nuit (bon noowee)= Good night

Bonjour.
Je m'appelle Julien

Can you say "hello, my name is _____" in French?

Money in France

In France they use the euro. The symbol for euro looks like this:

The French Flag Never Changes.....Or Does it?

This is the original flag

Then in 1976, the shade of blue was changed to match the European Union Flag.

In 2021, the President changed it back but didn't tell anyone! When people began to notice the change, many were outraged.

Which one do you like better?

The Weather in France

France has a mainly temperate climate. In other words, it never gets super hot or super cold...it's usually just nice. Northern and north-western France has a maritime climate with mild winters and warm summers. Central northern France has colder winters and slightly warmer summers, with Paris having a mean annual temperature of 13°C and a seasonal range of ±8°C.

The warmest place in France is the French Riviera coast in Southern France. With average summer temperatures well above 30C (80F) and long dry summers and warm springs and autumns, and mild winters, the South of France is the place to experience the best climate in France throughout the year.

The French Riviera

Paris averages 15 snow days a year, but they rarely get more than a dusting.

The Population of France

More than 67 MILLION people live in France. That's almost twice as many people as there are in Canada!

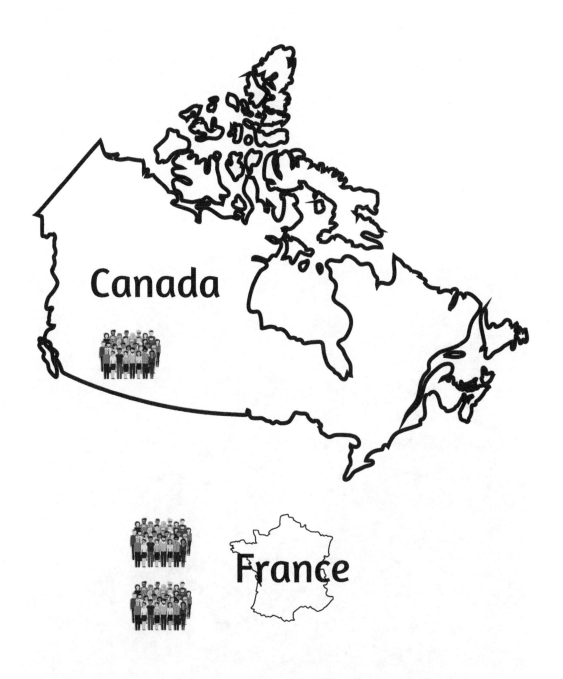

As seen in these pictures, France is much smaller than Canada, yet twice as many people live in France, probably because the climate in France is so nice compared to the colder Canadian weather.

What Kind of Homes do French People Live in?

68% of the French population
live in a single house.

What Kind of Homes do French People Live in?

22% live in a large apartment building.

What Kind of Homes do French People Live in?

10% live in a small apartment building with less than ten apartments.

How is School Different in France?

French school days are usually much longer, beginning at 8 a.m. and ending at 5 or 6 p.m. — except on Wednesdays, which end at noon. Like the American system, school is closed on the weekends. Lunch period is an hour-and-a-half long. Students in high school have the choice to have lunch outside of school, but the majority eat from the school menu

Currently, education is required for all children, but not attendance at a school. If a family decides to homeschool, the parents must declare they are homeschooling and are regularly visited by school inspectors to ensure the children are being educated to the same level as their peers. Today some 50,000 children are homeschooled in France. As of 2021, there are still arguments between the government and parents about the rules around homeschooling.

Elementary Schools in France

1 2 3 Soleil!

School kids get three recess breaks a day. Two short ones, then a long one after lunch. During recess, a popular game is called 1 2 3 Soleil (pronounced so-lay and means sun). If you're familiar with red-light, green-light, it's basically the same thing.

Two or more players can play 1 2 3 Soleil. One player is called La Sentinelle (the guard). La Sentinelle stands with his back to the other players and can't look at them. The other players start in a line, far away from La Sentinelle, and then they have to get as close to La Sentinelle as possible.

The other players can only advance while La Sentinelle isn't looking, and they must freeze in place when he turns around. To do this, La Sentinelle calls "un, deux, trois" (one, two, three) with his back turned, then yells "soleil!" when he turns around. This is when everyone freezes. If La Sentinelle catches them move, they are out.

The first player to avoid being out and who touches La Sentinelle, is the winner, and then that player becomes the new La Sentinelle.

Public Transit in France

You can get around pretty quickly in France, and pretty cheaply too. France has one of the best and fastest train services in the world. The prices are different depending on how far in advance you book. But if you take the train a lot, you can buy a monthly pass for under 100 euros.

Prefer the bus? There are several cities in France where riding the bus is completely free! The city governments argue that giving its citizens free bus service will help the economy and the environment. But so far, Paris still charges for the bus.

If you prefer to ride in a car but don't own one, and a taxi is too expensive, France allows ride-sharing. You sign up on an app and post where you want to go, and another person might post that he has a car and will drive you there. You agree on the price and decide on your pickup point. This service has a funny name. It's called Blablacar. This service started in Paris in 2006 and is now available in nine European countries.

The Landscapes of France

Most people immediately think of Paris when they hear about France. But did you know that France is made up of 25% forests and 50% countryside or farmland?

Forests

Countryside

Lakes

Mountains

Cities

Beaches

The French Alps

The Alps is a mountain range in Europe that stretches about 1,200 kilometres across eight countries: Monaco, France, Switzerland, Italy, Liechtenstein, Austria, Germany and Slovenia.

The largest mountain in the Alps is called Mont Blanc (white mountain). Although the top of the mountain is technically in France, they signed an agreement with Italy that says the mountain is "owned" equally between both countries.

Wild Animals That Live in France

wolf

lynx

chamois

Wild Animals That Live in France

wild boar

genet

bear

golden eagle

The Biggest Industries in France

Manufacturing & Technology

Agriculture

Transport

Energy

Tourism

France is the Most Visited Country in the World

The Palace of Versailles

The Palace was the home to King Louis XIV (the fourteenth) and was built in 1634. There are 2,300 rooms inside!

The building started as a small hunting lodge, but the King replaced that with a house between 1631-1634. Then he kept expanding it between 1661 and 1715.

In 1789, the royal family moved to Paris and left the Palace abandoned. When Napoleon Bonapart took over France, he used the Palace as his summer residence from 1810 - 1814.

It wasn't until the 1830s that the Palace was finally restored and turned into a museum of Frech history.

Today, the Palace is a designated Unesco World Heritage Site and is one of the most visited museums in the world, with an estimated 15 million visitors each year.

The French Revolution

The French Revolution began when the people of France got angry with King Louis XVI (the 16th). It seems the King and his family lived lavishly while raising taxes to pay for it all. The King was also generous to his friends in England and the United States. He helped to fund wars in both those countries. Meanwhile, the people of France had to keep paying higher taxes and couldn't afford to eat.

When the people had enough, the uprising started. By this time, the throne was headed by the late King's wife, Queen Marie Antoinette (1755 - 1793).

Napoleon Bonaparte (1769 - 1821) was a young man very interested in politics and philosophy. He quickly moved his way up the ranks and became army commander.

The monarchy was abolished during the French Revolution in 1792, and the King no longer ruled France. In 1804, at age 35, Napoleon Bonaparte crowned himself Emperor of France.

Is Paris Haunted?

Some visitors and museum workers believe that a mummy named Belphegor haunts the hallways of a famous Museum. Since the building dates back to 1190, this wouldn't be surprising.

The gardens on which the museum is built are also believed to be haunted by a ghost who appears red. He's been spotted by multiple individuals and is described as "totally unthreatening" — good to know!

Speaking of Haunted.....
Introducing the Story of the Catacombs!

As Paris grew into its role as a major European city, it eventually ran into a significant problem: by the 17th century, enough people had lived and died in Paris that its cemeteries were overflowing, overstuffed with graves to the point when corpses, at times became uncovered.

Those living in the Les Halles neighbourhood near Les Innocents, the city's oldest and largest cemetery were among the first to complain, reporting the cemetery exuded a strong smell of decomposing flesh—even perfume stores claimed they couldn't do business because of the off-putting smell.

The king wanted to move the bodies out of the city, but the church argued and said the bodies should not be touched. This argument lasted for 17 years! Then in 1780, a prolonged spring rain caused a wall around Les Innocents to collapse, spilling rotting corpses into a neighbouring property. The church really couldn't argue anymore after that! The city needed a better place to put its dead.

The solution was to move the bodies to old tunnels that had existed beneath the streets of Paris since the 13th century. By the time these burials ended, 6 million Parisians' bones had reached their final resting place in the city's catacombs.

World War II - France

On May 10, 1940, Hitler and the Nazi party of Germany invaded France. They occupied France for four years.

But France had many friends in the world, so on June 6, 1944, British, American, and Canadian troops planned a secret attack on the shores of Normandy and won France back. This day is known as D-Day. You might ask, what does the D in D-Day stand for: It stands for Day. That's right, D-Day means Day Day.

When a country has other countries as friends, they are called allies. Besides the UK, Canada and the United States, France had many allies who helped them regain their independence, including Australia, Belgium, the Netherlands, Greece, New Zealand, Norway, Rhodesia and Poland.

To make sure a war like this never happens again, NATO (The North Atlantic Treaty Organisation) was formed after World War II. The founding countries were Belgium, Canada, Denmark, France, Iceland, Italy, Luxembourg, the Netherlands, Norway, Portugal, the United Kingdom, and the United States.

Since then, 18 more countries have joined (including Germany) to become the most powerful allied group in the world.

Mont St Michel

Another famous tourist attraction is Mont St Michel in Normandy. It was built in the 8th century, and more than three million people from around the world visit every year.

When the tides rise each day, Mont St Michel becomes an island. In recent years, however, they built a permanent road so people could visit throughout the day without worrying about the tides trapping them.

France is Also Famous for its Lavender Farms

Lavender has many properties:
it's an antiseptic that soothes
and helps heal scars. Its essential
oil works wonders to relieve an
itch or make a bath more
relaxing.

The best time to visit France's
lavender farms is from mid-June
to mid-July.

Top Exports

The top exports of France (things they make and sell to other countries) are planes, helicopters, cars, turbines and packaged medicine. Their biggest customers are Germany, the United States, Italy and Belgium.

Top Exports

The French export more wine than any other country in the world. It's because the climate is perfect for growing grapes. In 2020, France exported more than 29% of the wine in the world.

Fashion

France is the global capital of fashion. It's a major part of their reputation and their economy. Fashion production in France began in the 15th century, and the French are still known today as being at the forefront of current trends.

The French do not like to dress too casually when in public. They want to show off their style. In North America, "athleisure" is very common. But not in France! They save their sweats, leggings and t-shirts for the gym, not the grocery store.

The Environment

The French government has been working hard to become more environmentally friendly. In May 2021, they created a climate change bill. This bill tries to reduce greenhouse gases by:

- Prohibiting the expansion of airports and prohibiting new airports
- Banning open-air terrace heaters at outdoor cafes and restaurants
- requiring state-run schools to have a meatless menu at least one day per week
- Requiring all supermarkets to reduce their use of plastic

The Environment

In 2018, the government also made some unpopular decisions, including removing fossil fuel subsidies (a subsidy is when the government helps you pay for something). When this happened, gas prices soared. The people of France became outraged because many needed their cars to get to work, and the cost of gas was not affordable anymore.

Protests in the streets became known as the Yellow Vest Protests. These protests were severe and caused much upset within the country. A survey showed that more than 70% of the French supported the yellow vest protests.

To make amends, the President promised to reduce taxes and increase the minimum wage for workers.

So you can see that sometimes when you try to fix one problem (the environment), other issues can result (like the cost of gas).

Famous French Inventions

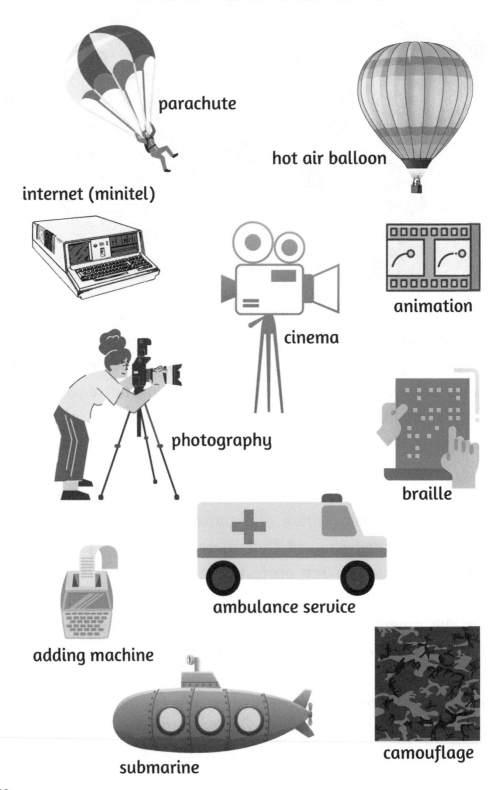

parachute

hot air balloon

internet (minitel)

cinema

animation

photography

braille

ambulance service

adding machine

submarine

camouflage

Animation

The first animated cartoon with an actual plot was Fantasmagorie by Émile Cohl. It premiered at the Théâtre du Gymnase in Paris on August 17 1908. Drawn on paper and shot onto negative film in what became the traditional creation method, the film shows a stick figure moving through space and interacting with various shape-shifting objects. Cohl's movies and those that followed were highly successful, and he continued to pioneer new techniques.

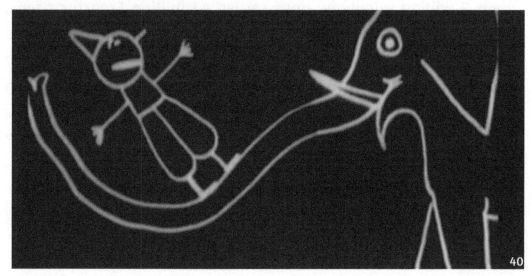

Minitel - The Beginning of the Internet

In the late 1970's France had to face the fact that its telephone network was one of the worst in the industrialized world. Fewer than 7 million telephone lines served 47 million French citizens. Technology was advancing fast in the US, and France was becoming embarrassed. Government researchers Simon Nora and Alain Minc created a solution called "telematics"—a combination of telecommunications and informatics. They outlined a plan for digitizing the telephone network, adding a layer of interactive Teletext video technology, and providing entrepreneurs with an open platform for innovation.

In 1991, most Americans had not yet heard of the internet. But all of France was online, buying, selling, gaming, and chatting, all thanks to Minitel.

Minitel was a tiny computer terminal. It had a screen, a keyboard, and a modem—but not a microprocessor. Instead of computing on its own, Minitel connected to remote services via uplinks, like a 1960s mainframe or a modern Google Chromebook. Terminals were given out, for free, to every French telephone subscriber by the state (which also ran the phone company).

Minitel was a huge success. With free terminals at home or work, people in France could connect to more than 25,000 online services long before the world wide web had even been invented. With a Minitel, you could read the news, engage in multi-player interactive gaming, grocery shop for same-day delivery, submit natural language requests like "reserve theatre tickets in Paris," purchase the tickets using a credit card, remotely control thermostats and other home appliances, manage a bank account, chat, and date. All this before the internet was even invented!

Amusement Parks in France

There are a total of 33 amusement parks throughout France and a total of eight theme and leisure parks in Paris.

Other Fun Places to Go

Besides amusement parks, you'll find many other fun places in France. They have laser games, escape rooms, science centres, water parks and children's museums.

Bastille Day

Bastille Day falls on July 14 and is a major holiday in France. They celebrate with fireworks, parades and parties.

Bastille Day celebrates the storming of the Bastille on July 14, 1789.

The Bastille was a prison. Some people in jail were writers and creative thinkers. The king locked them up without a trial.

By 1789 there were only seven prisoners left. These seven prisoners were four forgers, two men who had a mental health conditions and one man who was an aristocrat (wealthy and important). But the people were so angry, they shot cannons and fought until the prisoners were freed. One of the prisoners refused to leave until he ate his dinner.

To this day, the people of France celebrate their victory of that day when they freed the prisoners in the Bastille.

Bastille Day
July 14
Vive La France!

Christmas Traditions

There are a few differences between the way the French celebrate Christmas compared to North American Christmas.

In North America, Christmas colours are red and green. In France, they don't assign any colours to Christmas.

Christmas cards and carolling are not a part of the celebrations in France.

Although Christmas gifts from Santa Claus (Pere Noel) are opened on Christmas morning, in France, gifts between family members are exchanged on Christmas Eve.

Fun Fact About April Fools' Day

April Fools' Day started in 1582 when France switched from the Julian calendar to the Gregorian calendar (the one we use today). In the Julian Calendar, the new year begins with the spring equinox around April 1.

People who were slow to get the news or failed to recognise that the start of the new year had moved to January 1 and continued to celebrate it during the last week of March through April 1 became the butt of jokes and hoaxes and were called "April fools." These pranks included having paper fish placed on their backs and being referred to as "Poisson d'avril" (April fish) because they were gullible or "easily caught".

Even today, if you are in France on April 1, you'll see children tape paper fish on as many adults' backs as possible, then run away yelling "poisson d'avril!"

Customs When You Are Invited to Someone's Home

If you are ever invited to someone's home in France, there are a few things you should be aware of, so share these tips with your parents:

Always arrive at least 15-20 minutes late to a dinner party. If you show up on time, you might catch the host still preparing. Being a little late is seen as offering the host a little extra time in case they need it.

It is impolite to bring wine to a dinner party. It is assumed that the host took special care in selecting the wine, so if you bring some, you are implying the host doesn't know what they are doing. However, bringing a small gift like chocolates or flowers is considered polite.

In France, most residents practice the double kiss greeting, i.e. a glancing kiss on each cheek. And, there are regions, particularly in northern France, where people favour four kisses – even five. This can catch visitors off-guard, as can potential awkwardness around which cheek to present first!

Customs When You Are Invited to Someone's Home

The French prefer to drink water and soft drinks at room temperature or lightly chilled. Of course, you'll have to ask for ice if you want it.

In France, bread is often placed directly on the table rather than a plate, just so you know.

Say Cheese!

The French are one of the highest consumers of cheese in the world. The average person in France eats 26.7 kg (almost 59 pounds) of cheese yearly!

Every region in France supports a large population of milk-giving animals, which provide the raw material for French cheese. Therefore, there are more than 400 French cheese varieties listed in France.

 96% of French people eat cheese

 only 4% seldom or never eat cheese

 47% of French people eat cheese every day

With a Side of Snails?

Absolutely! The French eat 25,000 tons of snails each year. That's an average of 500 snails per person! But in France, snails are known as "escargot" and pronounced es-car-go. Sounds much classier n'est pas? (isn't that so?).

What Other Foods Are Popular in France?

bread and pastries

seafood

magret de canard (duck, salad and potatoes)

What Other Foods Are Popular in France?

soups and potage (boiled vegetables made into a creamy soup)

omelette

What About Breakfast?

In France, kids usually have toast or cereal for breakfast, but with a few differences.

There isn't a huge variety of cereals in French supermarkets like there are in the U.S., and their cereals are less sugary.

What About Breakfast?

As for toast, they might put butter or jam on it, but not peanut butter. Peanut butter is sold in grocery stores, but the French buy it to cook Asian dishes, not sandwiches or toast.

French people also enjoy a croissant for a light breakfast.

Goûter

French children tend to eat dinner at 7:30 or 8 pm. So it's common for them to have a big lunch and then eat again around 4:00 pm. They call the snack goûter (pronounced Goo-tee). It's usually something sweet (like a piece of cake) as a treat to have before homework.

French Cooking Schools

If you ever want to become a famous chef someday, you should attend a cooking school in France. Chefs who want to become the very best should have at least some mention of a French culinary school on their resumé.

For amateur chefs, you can find weekend cooking classes all over France. The French take pride in their reputation of being world-class cooks. You can even find a "knifing class" where you learn how to chop vegetables like a real chef.

The Most Popular Sports in France

1. Football (soccer)
2. Tennis
3. Horse Riding
4. Basketball
5. Judo – Jujitsu
6. Handball
7. Rugby
8. Golf
9. Canoe – Kayak
10. Sailing

The Tour de France

The Tour de France is the world's most famous bicycle race. The first race was in 1903. There were only 60 racers.

Today the race has 21 stages and takes 23 days to complete (2 are rest days). The racers are in teams of 9, and there are 22 teams for 198 racers. The race covers 3,500 kilometres and runs every summer.

A typical bicycle in the Tour de France is worth 11,500 euros or 13,000 dollars.

Olympic Standing

Even though they are not in the top ten most popular sports, France usually wins the most medals in fencing and cycling when competing at the Olympics.

More French Fun Facts

The French Can Be a Superstitious Bunch

Here are some common superstitions in France:

Never leave a baguette or loaf of bread upside down on a table. If you do, you will invite hunger into the house.

If you're moving into a new house, be sure to bring the table in first so it will bring you good luck.

Stepping in poo with your right foot is bad luck. But if you step in with your left foot, that's good luck.

Never give anyone chrysanthemums. They will bring bad luck to the receiver.

10 Funniest Laws in France

Every country has some strange laws still on the books. France is no exception. Although they are no longer enforced, they remain as laws today. Here are ten of the funniest:

1. Snails must have their own ticket to ride on the train.

2. You can't name your pig Napoleon.

3. Don't kiss in a French train station.

4. Women who want to dress like a man must first ask the police.

5. You must listen to French music. 40% of the music on the radio must be by French artists.

6. School cafeterias cannot serve ketchup.

7. You must say bonjour when in the town hall in Lheraule.

8. You can write a cheque on toilet paper.

9. You can divorce your husband if he watches too much football.

10. It is illegal to fly over or land flying saucers in the southern French town of Chateauneuf-du-Pape.

Pets in France

French people love their animals. In France, the most popular pets are fish, with approximately 36 million. The second most popular pets are cats, with 10.7 million and dogs, with 7.8 million. 25% of all homes have a dog, and about 33% have at least one cat.

Dogs are Welcome Almost Everywhere in France

Shops, hotels, bars, restaurants, as long as your dog is well-behaved, he is welcome pretty much everywhere.

Come Minette!

Minette is the most popular cat name in France. So be careful; if you call out "viens Minette!" (come Minette) in France, you might get more than you can handle.

After learning so much about France, I guess you can understand why it is the world's most visited country. France is beautiful; the people are warm and friendly, the food is fantastic, and it's a very safe country for a family to visit.

Acknowldegements:

French Overseas Territories Attribution - ShareAlike 4.0 International
"Haguenau Forest" by noirdenoir67 is licensed under CC0 1.0

"Lac du Bourget" by *pascal* is licensed under CC BY 2.0

"Mont Blanc" by *rboed* is licensed under CC BY 2.0

"Falaise d'Amont, Etretat, Normandie" by travelourplanet.com is licensed under CC BY 2.0

"Fantasmagorie" by www.brevestoriadelcinema.org is licensed under CC PDM 1.0

"Fantasmagorie" by www.brevestoriadelcinema.org is licensed under CC PDM 1.0

"Yves Saint Laurent - Le Smoking - Danielle Sauvajeon - 1968" by wufonseca is licensed under CC BY-ND 2.0

"Chanel Iman at Christian Dior Haute Couture Fashion Show" by chanelimanphotos is licensed under CC BY 2.0

"Minitel 2" by zigazou76 is licensed under CC BY 2.0

"Tux sur un Minitel" by zigazou76 is licensed under CC BY 2.0

"Paris Catacombs" by levork is licensed under CC BY-SA 2.0

"File:Ecole Jean Macé (2).jpg" by Philippe Alès is licensed under CC BY-SA 4.0

"File:Ecole Jean Macé Le Havre (1).jpg" by Philippe Alès is licensed under CC BY-SA 4.0

About the Author

Collette Valliear is a world-traveller and proud G-Mom to Julien and Beau! She loves to write about travelling and is excited to help inspire others to embrace their inner vagabond. Collette has visited all seven continents and looks forward to taking her grandsons on some epic adventures one day! They love to request books and contribute new ideas often. Collette, a former property manager in Toronto, Canada, turned her retirement into a new chapter of adventure and creativity!

To see more books by Meonatrip, scan the QR code below.

Please leave an honest review on Amazon; it will go a long way to creating more books like this one.

MEONATRIP

2021

Made in the USA
Coppell, TX
25 April 2023

16061098R00044